THE SECOND OFFICIAL
I HATE CATS BOOK

Also by Skip Morrow

THE OFFICIAL I HATE CATS BOOK
THE OFFICIAL I HATE CATS CALENDAR 1982

As Illustrator

THE 300 POUND CAT, by Rosamond Dauer

THE SECOND OFFICIAL
I HATE CATS BOOK

Skip Morrow

An Owl Book

HOLT, RINEHART AND WINSTON • NEW YORK

"Little Jesus watches over drunks, babies, and Skipper Morrow."
—BERYL MORROW

For Mom and Dad

Published by Holt, Rinehart and Winston, 383 Madison Avenue, New York, New York 10017.
Published simultaneously in Canada by Holt, Rinehart and Winston of Canada, Limited.

Library of Congress Catalog Card Number: 81-47461
ISBN: 0-03-059359-X

Printed in the United States of America
3   5   7   9   10   8   6   4

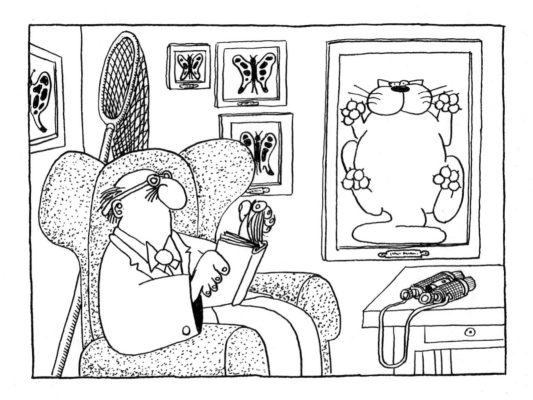

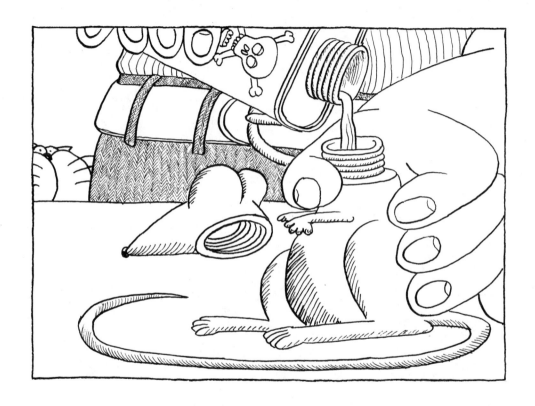

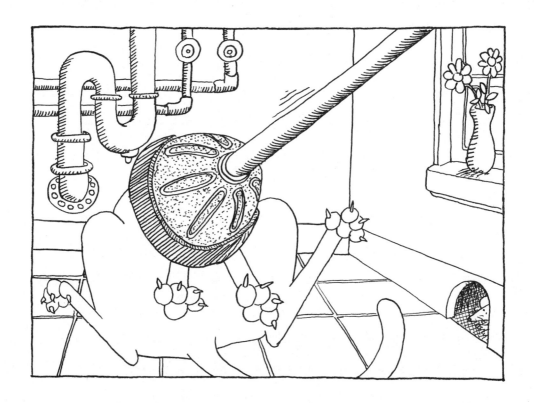